UNIT 3

RELATIONSHIPS AND COMMUNICATION ACTIVITIES

PATRICIA RIZZO TONER

Includes 90 ready-to-use worksheets for grades 7-12

Just for the HEALTH of It!
Health Curriculum Activities Library

THE CENTER FOR APPLIED
RESEARCH IN EDUCATION
West Nyack, New York 10995

Library of Congress Cataloging-in-Publication Data

Toner, Patricia Rizzo, 1952– .
    Relationships and communication activities / Patricia Rizzo Toner.
      p.   cm.—(Just for the health of it! ; unit 3)
    Includes 90 ready-to-use activities.
    ISBN 0-87628-847-6
    1. Interpersonal relations—Study and teaching (Secondary)
    2. Interpersonal communication—Study and teaching (Secondary)
    3. Activity programs in education.   I. Title. II. Series.
    HM132.T663   1993
    302′.071′2—dc20
                                       93-9074
                                       CIP

The source for many of the clip art images in this book is
Presentation Task Force which is a registered trademark of
New Vision Technologies, Inc., copyright 1991.

Printed in the United States of America

10   9   8   7   6   5

ISBN 0-87628-847-6

**THE CENTER FOR APPLIED RESEARCH
IN EDUCATION**
West Nyack, NY 10994

On the World Wide Web at http://www.phdirect.com

DEDICATION

To my son, Danny Toner of Holland, Pennsylvania

May we always be able to communicate openly
with one another and maintain a close relationship.

ABOUT THE AUTHOR

Patricia Rizzo Toner, M.Ed., has taught Health and Physical Education in the Council Rock School District, Holland, PA, for over 19 years, and she has also coached gymnastics and field hockey. She is the co-author of three books: *What Are We Doing in Gym Today?, You'll Never Guess What We Did in Gym Today!,* and *How to Survive Teaching Health.* Besides her work as a teacher, Pat is also a freelance cartoonist. A member of the American Alliance for Health, Physical Education, Recreation and Dance, Pat received the Hammond Service Award, the Marianna G. Packer Book Award and was named to *Who's Who Among Students in American Colleges and Universities,* as well as *Who's Who in American Education.*

ACKNOWLEDGMENTS

Thanks to Colleen Leh and Barb Snyder of Holland Junior High, Holland, Pennsylvania, for reviewing each activity and providing valuable feedback.

ABOUT <u>JUST FOR THE HEALTH OF IT!</u>

Just for the Health of It! was developed to give you, the health teacher, new ways to present difficult-to-teach subjects and to spark your students' interest in day-to-day health classes. It includes over 540 ready-to-use activities organized for your teaching convenience into six separate, self-contained units, each focused on a major area of health education.

Each unit provides ninety classroom-tested activities printed in a full-page format and ready to be photocopied as many times as needed for student use. Many of the activities are illustrated with cartoon figures to enliven the material and help inject a touch of humor into the health curriculum.

The following briefly describes each of the six units in the series:

Unit 1: *Consumer Health and Safety Activities* helps students recognize advertising techniques, compare various products and claims, understand consumer rights, distinguish between safe and dangerous items, become familiar with safety rules, and more.

Unit 2: *Diet and Nutrition Activities* focuses on basic concepts and skills such as the four food groups, caloric balance or imbalance, the safety of diets, food additives, and vitamin deficiency diseases.

Unit 3: *Relationships and Communication Activities* explores topics such as family relationships, sibling rivalry, how to make friends, split-level communications, assertiveness and aggressiveness, dating, divorce, and popularity.

Unit 4: *Sex Education Activities* teaches about the male and female reproductive systems, various methods of contraception ranging from abstinence to mechanical and chemical methods, sexually transmitted diseases, the immune system, pregnancy, fetal development, childbirth, and more.

Unit 5: *Stress-Management and Self-Esteem Activities* examines the causes and signs of stress and teaches ways of coping with it. Along with these, the unit focuses on various elements of building self-esteem such as appearance, values, self-concept, success and confidence, personality, and character traits.

Unit 6: *Substance Abuse Prevention Activities* deals with the use and abuse of tobacco, alcohol, and other drugs and examines habits ranging from occasional use to addiction. It also promotes alternatives to drug use by examining peer pressure situations, decision-making, and where to seek help.

To help you mix and match activities from the series with ease, all of the activities in each unit are designated with two letters to represent each resource as follows: Sex Education (SE), Substance Abuse Prevention (SA), Relationships and Communication (RC), Stress-Management and Self-Esteem (SM), Diet and Nutrition (DN), and Consumer Health and Safety (CH).

About Unit 3

Relationships and Communication Activities provides you with many ideas for your Communication, Relationships, and Family Living units.

This resource is designed for teachers who are looking to enhance their collection of activities and ideas. It contains two main teaching tools:

- reproducibles designed for quick copying to hand out to students; and
- activities that give you ideas, games, and instructions to supplement your classroom presentation.

Use these aids to introduce a communication, relationships, or family living unit, to increase interest at any given point in a lesson, or to reinforce what students have learned.

An at-a-glance table of contents provides valuable help by supplying general and specific topic heads with a complete list of activities and reproducibles. The ninety activities that make up this resource focus on the following important elements of a consumer health and safety unit:

Family Relationships. This section contains handouts and activities highlighting the family as a unit, family rules and responsibilities, parent-teen relationships, and sibling rivalry.

Friendship. This section focuses on the qualities of friendship, conformity, and peer relationships.

Dating and Marriage. Handouts and activities covered in this section include qualities you look for in a mate, teen marriage, teen parenting, dating relationships, and thought-provoking discussions.

Communication. Important elements of communication are covered in this section, such as, body language, listening skills, assertiveness, and speaking skills.

Group Dynamics. This section focuses on cooperation, brainstorming, and compromise.

Communication Breakdown. Activities and handouts deal with the causes of poor communication.

Conflict Resolution. Anger, conflict situations, and steps to resolving conflicts are highlighted.

The reproducibles and activities are designated *RC*, representing the Relationships and Communication component of the *Health Curriculum Activities Library*. These games, activities, puzzles, charts, and worksheets can be put directly into your lesson plans. They can be used on an individual basis or as a whole-class activity.

I hope you will enjoy using these activities as much as I have.

Patricia Rizzo Toner

CONTENTS

SKILLS AND METHODS OF COMMUNICATION   49

Speaking Skills

GROUP DYNAMICS

Cooperation

Brainstorming

Compromise

COMMUNICATION BREAKDOWN   **85**

Mixed Messages

Eye Contact

Poor Communication

Conflict Resolution

FAMILY RELATIONSHIPS

- **The Family Unit**

- **Family Responsibilities**

- **Parent-Teen Relationships**

- **Parent-Teen Conflicts**

- **Siblings**

ACTIVITY 1: FAMILY TREE

Concept/ Description: Investigating your family tree can teach you about yourself and your family.

Objective: To draw a picture of family members, attach them to a family tree, and write a brief biography of each person.

Materials: Family Photos Sheet (RC-1)
Family Tree Sheet (RC-2)
Pens or pencils
Paste or glue
Scissors

Directions:
1. Give each student a Family Tree sheet and a Family Photos sheet.

2. Have students draw a picture of each family member in the frames on the Family Photos sheet. Pictures can be as detailed as they wish.

3. Students are to cut out the pictures and paste them onto the Family Tree sheet. **Note:** Be sensitive to the fact that some students may have lost a parent or grandparent. One way to handle this is to speak to the child privately and ask if he or she wishes to write what is remembered about that person, or if he or she would prefer to be excused from the activity.

4. Have students write brief comments under or next to each picture highlighting the family member's positive qualities or accomplishments.

5. Have students draw a star next to each quality they also possess.

6. Display the finished trees in the class.

"This is my family's tree!!"

FAMILY PHOTOS

FAMILY TREE (RC-2)

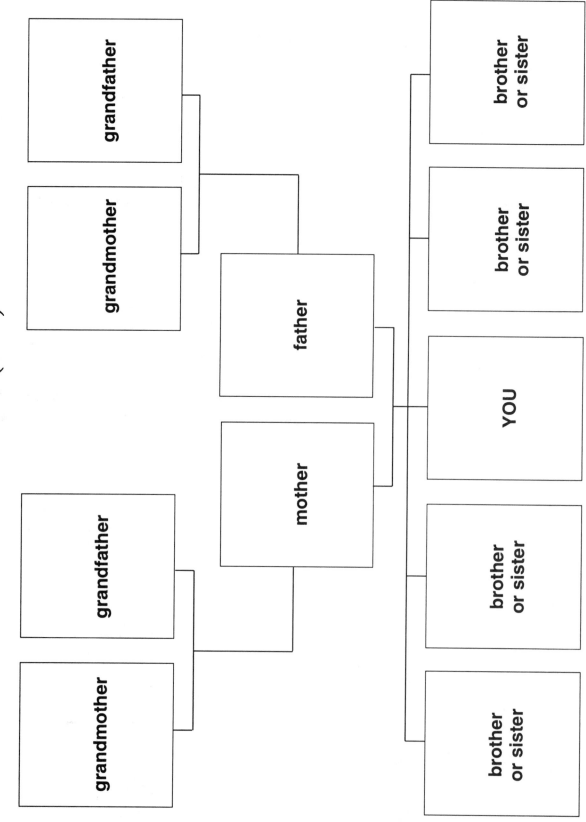

ACTIVITY 2: THANK YOU, MRS. CLEAVER

Concept/ Description: Television often portrays family life unrealistically.

Objective: To determine which television shows are unrealistic in their portrayal of family life and why they are unrealistic.

Materials: TV Families sheet (RC-3)
Pens or pencils

Directions:
1. Give each student a TV Families sheet to complete at home.
2. Ask students to watch a show in which a family is featured. The show can be from the present or the past. Ask students to consider how realistic each family is as they watch the show. Analyze the show by filling out the worksheet and bring it back to class.
3. Compile a list of television shows watched and ask students to share their thoughts as to how accurately each show depicted the typical family.
4. Discuss what was realistic and what was unrealistic and why.
5. Did any shows feature families in financial trouble, abusive families, parents who are divorced or separated, alcoholism or other drug abuse, or homelessness? Why might certain television shows steer clear of these topics while others address the issues?
6. Discuss.

"Hi children!...Welcome home from school! Let's have some milk and home-baked chocolate-chip cookies. Then we can all have a sing-along before Dad gets home, okay?"

Name _____ **Date** _____

TV FAMILIES (RC-3)

DIRECTIONS: Watch any TV show that features a family and answer the questions below:

1. Name of television show: _____

2. What type of show was your TV show
   (comedy, drama, series, special, etc.)? _____

3. What was realistic about the way
   the TV family was portrayed? _____

   _____

   _____

   _____

4. What was unrealistic about the
   way the TV family was portrayed? _____

   _____

   _____

   _____

5. Check any of these family problems that your show addressed or depicted:

☐ parents fighting   ☐ alcoholism or other drug abuse

☐ siblings fighting   ☐ infidelity

☐ financial problems   ☐ homelessness

☐ loss of job   ☐ teen-parent conflicts

☐ divorce or separation   ☐ latchkey children

☐ abuse   ☐ death or serious illness

Name _____ **Date** _____

FAMILY RULES (RC-4)

DIRECTIONS: Every family has certain rules that family members are expected to follow. There are often consequences for failure to abide by the rules. Write down some of your family rules and the consequences.

Rules	Consequences
Dinner is served at 6:00, and we must be in on time.	**Make your own dinner if late without calling.**

Name _____ **Date** _____

JOB SEARCH (RC-5)

DIRECTIONS: At the top of each column, place the name of a family member who lives at home. Then, write an *X* under each column to show the jobs and chores each family member has. Who has the most responsibilities?

FAMILY MEMBERS:						
JOBS:						
Cooking						
Cleaning bedrooms						
Mowing the lawn						
Gardening						
Car repairs/service						
Grocery shopping						
Transportation						
Paying the bills						
Laundry						
Doing the dishes						
Cleaning bathroom						
Mopping floors						
Vacuuming						
Taking out the						
trash						
Feeding pets						
Grooming pets						
Washing car						
Washing windows						
Earning money						
Setting the table						
Clearing the table						
Dusting						
Walking pets						
Making beds						
Shoveling snow						
Raking leaves						

ACTIVITY 3: I KNOW YOU

Concept/ Description: Students and parents will compare charts to see how well they know each other.

Objective: To see how many answers match when comparing charts.

Materials: How Well Do You Know Your Parents? sheet (RC-6)
How Well Do You Know Your Child? sheet (RC-7)
Pens or pencils

Directions:
1. Give each student a How Well Do You Know Your Parents? sheet to complete during class.

2. Ask them to write down their answers and then, write down what they think their parents will say.

3. Next, give each student a How Well Do You Know Your Child? sheet to take home for their parents to complete.

4. Have students compare their papers to their parent's papers and place a circle around each answer that matches.

5. Count up the number of matches. How well do you know each other?

6. Discuss in class.

Name _____   **Date** _____

HOW WELL DO YOU KNOW YOUR PARENTS? (RC-6)

DIRECTIONS: Fill in the chart for yourself and for one parent. Give a How Well Do You Know Your Child? chart to your mother, father, or guardian to complete. Compare your chart with your parent's chart. How well do you know each other?

TOPIC	YOU	PARENT
Favorite TV Show		
Favorite Subject in School		
Favorite Sport to Play		
Favorite Foods		
Favorite Musical Group or Person		
Least Favorite Foods		
Least Favorite Subject in School		
Least Favorite Type of Music		
Favorite Free-Time Activity		
Least Favorite Chore		
Favorite Actor or Actress		
Favorite Book or Author		
Favorite Professional Sports Team		
Favorite Sport to Watch		
Thing That Makes You the Angriest		

Name _____ Date _____

HOW WELL DO YOU KNOW YOUR CHILD? (RC-7)

DIRECTIONS: Fill in the chart for yourself and for your child. Compare your chart with your child's chart. How well do you know each other?

©1993 by The Center for Applied Research in Education

TOPIC	YOU	CHILD
Favorite TV Show		
Favorite Subject in School		
Favorite Sport to Play		
Favorite Foods		
Favorite Musical Group or Person		
Least Favorite Foods		
Least Favorite Subject in School		
Least Favorite Type of Music		
Favorite Free-Time Activity		
Least Favorite Chore		
Favorite Actor or Actress		
Favorite Book or Author		
Favorite Professional Sports Team		
Favorite Sport to Watch		
Thing That Makes You the Angriest		

PERFECT PARENTS (RC-8)

DIRECTIONS: No set of parents is perfect, but if you could have perfect parents, describe all of their qualities. If your parents are as close to perfect can be, describe the qualities they possess. Write the qualities around the pictures of the parents. Next to each quality, write the symbols of the codes that apply. The codes are listed in the box at the bottom of the page.

©1993 by The Center for Applied Research in Education

Codes:

+ **You possess this quality.**
M **Your mother possesses this quality.**
F **Your father possesses this quality.**
* **These are the three most important qualities of a good parent.**

Name _____   **Date** _____

NEW PARENTS (RC-9)

DIRECTIONS: If you could pick ANY two people in the world (other than your own parents) to be your parents, whom would you pick? Explain why, in detail.

Dad _____
Why:

Mom _____
Why:

ACTIVITY 4: FAMILY CIRCLE

**Concept/
Description:** Conflicts between parents and teenagers start for a variety of reasons.

Objective: To explore some of the reasons that conflicts arise between teenagers and their parents and to discuss strategies for resolving them.

Materials: Family Circle Cards (RC-10)
Paper
Pens or pencils

Directions:
1. Divide the class into eight groups and ask the group members to sit in a circle.

2. Have one group member choose a Family Circle card, then return to his or her group. Tell the group members the topic that was chosen.

3. Tell students they have 5 minutes to write down as many examples of conflict for the given category that they can think of. (For example, for the category of appearance, students might write: parents hate my long hair, parents don't like boys wearing earrings, teens want to wear jeans with holes in them to school and parents disapprove.)

4. When all groups have completed the task, have each group tell which category was chosen and give their examples.

5. Next, discuss the nature of these conflicts and ask students for ideas for resolving conflicts. Choose the best strategies and write them on the board.

FAMILY CIRCLE Cards (RC-10)

CONFLICT: **APPEARANCE**	*CONFLICT:* **HOMEWORK & SCHOOLWORK**
CONFLICT: **CHOICE OF FRIENDS**	*CONFLICT:* **BOYFRIEND OR GIRLFRIEND**
CONFLICT: **MUSIC & INTERESTS**	*CONFLICT:* **RULES & CURFEW**
CONFLICT: **CHORES & NEATNESS**	*CONFLICT:* **PHONE USE & TIME AWAY FROM FAMILY**

Name _____ Date _____

WHEN I WAS YOUR AGE... (RC-11)

DIRECTIONS: Listed below are some of the comments teenagers "hate" to hear from their parents and some of the comments parents "hate" to hear from their teenagers. Add your own to the list and then ask your parents to add to the list at the bottom. Bring your finished paper back to class. Discuss with a partner.

Parent comments teenagers "hate" to hear:

When I was your age...
Look at me when I'm speaking to you.
Stand up straight.
Tell me about your day.
Wipe that smile off your face!

Teenager comments parents "hate" to hear:

Everyone else is allowed to go!
You're so unfair!
You never let me do anything!
You never listen to my point of view!

ACTIVITY 5: BIRTH ORDER

Concept/ Description: Birth order may affect how a person interprets his or her place in the family.

Objective: To list and discuss the advantages and disadvantages of various places in sibling birth order.

Materials: Birth Order sheet (RC-12)
Chalkboard
Chalk
Pens or pencils

Directions:
1. Give each student a Birth Order sheet to fill out.
2. Ask students to list their order of birth (oldest, youngest, only child, middle child, second born, etc.).
3. Have students fill out the advantages and disadvantages of their position in the family. Then, place students in groups according to similar birth order.
4. Ask each group to compile one list of advantages and list them on the chalkboard for all to see. Discuss as a class.
5. Repeat the same process for disadvantages. Write composite lists on the board and discuss.
6. Explain that birth order does not determine a child's personality, but it can affect how children feel about themselves.

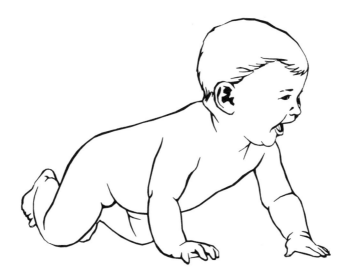

BIRTH ORDER (RC-12)

DIRECTIONS: List your birth order (oldest, second child, middle child, only child, twin, youngest). Then, fill out the chart listing all the advantages and disadvantages of your place in the family.

Birth Order_____

ADVANTAGES	DISADVANTAGES

SIBLING RIVALRY (RC-13)

DIRECTIONS: Sibling rivalry is the natural arguing and fighting that occurs among many brothers and sisters as they are growing up. Different siblings use different methods to try to influence or control each other. Look at the examples listed below and add others to the boxes. Then, answer the questions at the bottom of the page.

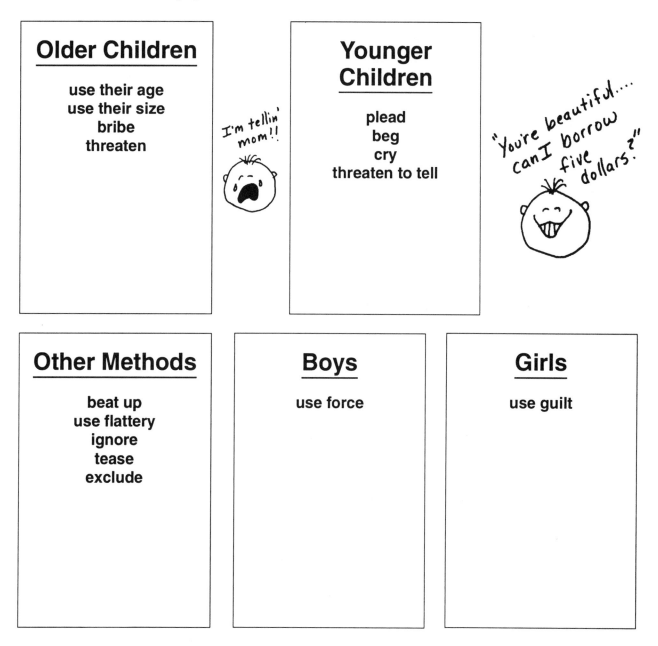

Older Children

use their age
use their size
bribe
threaten

I'm tellin' mom!!

Younger Children

plead
beg
cry
threaten to tell

"You're beautiful.... can I borrow five dollars?"

Other Methods

beat up
use flattery
ignore
tease
exclude

Boys

use force

Girls

use guilt

In your opinion, which of the methods listed have the best chance of making siblings change? Which ones are least effective?

REVENGE (RC-14)

DIRECTIONS: Read the story, then answer the questions.

> One afternoon two sisters played cards in the family room. What started as a friendly game quickly turned into an argument with shouts of "You're cheating!" and a barrage of verbal insults. Finally, Cindy, the older sister, couldn't stand it any longer and pushed her sister out of her chair. Diane, the younger sister, fell and injured her wrist.
>
> Cindy was immediately filled with regret and afraid that she'd hurt her sister. Diane's wrist was sprained and needed ice but was probably okay. Diane quickly seized the opportunity.
>
> Diane threatened to call their parents if Cindy didn't let her wear her new jeans to school tomorrow. Cindy quickly agreed to the terms, fearing her parent's punishment. As she gave her sister her new jeans, Cindy knew she'd find an opportunity to get her revenge.

1. If you were Cindy, how would you react to Diane's blackmail?

2. If you were the girls' parents, what rules would you set about fighting?

3. As a parent, would you forbid all physical fighting?

4. Do you favor "an eye for an eye" philosophy of punishment? (Example: If Diane ruins Cindy's jeans, Cindy can ruin something of Diane's.) Why or why not?

5. If you had to make one rule that would make brothers and sisters get along better, what would it be?

Name _____   **Date** _____

SIBLING CONFLICT (RC-15)

DIRECTIONS: Below is a list of common areas of conflict between brothers and sisters. Add your own complaints to the list and discuss with a classmate.

1. Not enough privacy.

2. Borrowing clothes without permission.

3. Borrowing possessions without permission.

4. Uneven workload (chores).

5. Uneven privileges granted by parents.

6. Hogging the telephone.

7. Hogging the television.

8. Teasing.

9. Uneven amount of attention given by parents.

10.

11.

12.

13.

14.

15.

16.

17.

18.

FRIENDSHIP

- **Qualities of Friendship**

- **Conformity**

Name _____   **Date** _____

HOW WELL DO YOU KNOW YOUR FRIEND? (RC-16)

DIRECTIONS: Fill in the chart for yourself and for a friend. Compare your chart with your friend's chart. How well do you know each other?

TOPIC	YOU	FRIEND
Favorite TV Show		
Favorite Subject		
Favorite Sport		
Favorite Foods		
Favorite Musical Group or Person		
Least Favorite Foods		
Least Favorite Subject		
Least Favorite Musical Group or Person		
Favorite Free-Time Activity		
Least Favorite Chore		
Favorite Actor or Actress		
Favorite Book		
Favorite Professional Sports Team		
Pet Peeve		
Favorite Saying		

DESIGN THE "PERFECT FRIEND" (RC-17)

DIRECTIONS: If you could design the perfect friend, what qualities would he or she possess? Write the qualities you look for in a friend around the figures below. Then go back over your list and write an asterisk (*) next to the qualities YOU possess.

Name _____ **Date** _____

SUNDAY COMICS (RC-18)

DIRECTIONS: In the first set of boxes below, design a comic strip in which friends use poor communication skills. In the second set of boxes, design a comic strip showing friends using good communication skills. In the third set, show one friend being passive, one being aggressive, and one being assertive in resolving a difference.

Name _____   **Date** _____

MAY I QUOTE YOU? (RC-19)

DIRECTIONS: Look at the two quotes below and, in the boxes, write down what you think the quotes mean. How can these quotes be related to relationships? Discuss your thoughts with a partner.

"You don't have to blow out my candle to make yours glow brighter."

"The only way to have a friend is to be a friend."

ACTIVITY 6: FAD, BUT TRUE

**Concept/
Description:** Fads are an example of conformity. Conformity means to go along with the group.

Objective: To look at fads of the past and discuss conformity.

Materials: Fad, But True sheet (RC-20)
Pens or pencils

Directions:
1. Give each student a Fad, But True sheet.
2. Ask students to go to local libraries, or interview adults to try to get a list of fads that were popular during the times given.
3. Follow the activity with a discussion of fads and conformity.
4. Ask students if they agree with this statement: "Unless you conform in some ways, you are likely to be treated as an outsider." Why or why not? Discuss.
5. How can fads cause problems? Discuss.
6. How can conformity cause problems? Discuss.

"But, mom,
this hairdo is
the latest fad!!"

Name _____ Date _____

FAD, BUT TRUE (RC-20)

YEAR	FADS
1950s	**hula hoops** **'coon skin caps**
1960s	**peace signs** **bell-bottoms**
1970s	**go-go boots** **long sideburns**
1980s	**breakdancing** **parachute pants** **spiked hair**
1990s	**loose-fitting jeans** **"pumps" sneakers** **rap music**

SURROUNDED (RC-21)

DIRECTIONS: Groups provide a sense of belonging, help build confidence and self-esteem, and make certain activities enjoyable that a person might not do alone. Make a list of all the groups to which you have belonged by writing the name of the group in the proper category below.

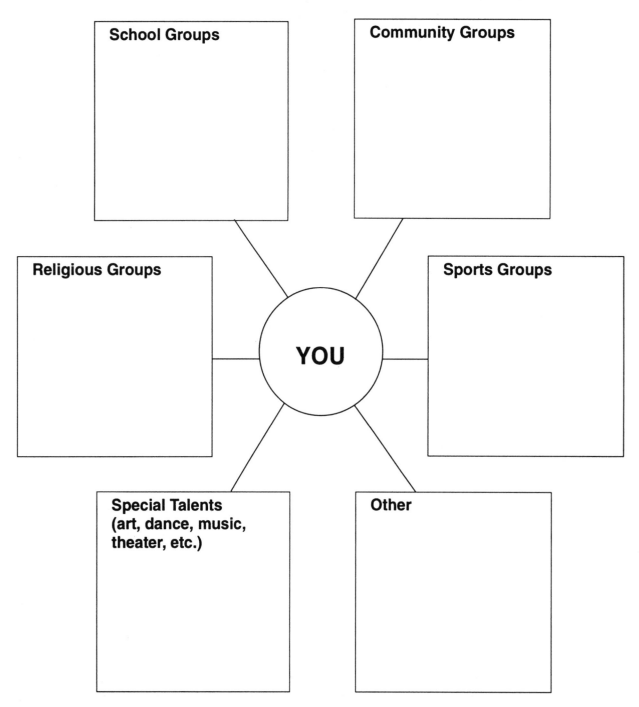

School Groups

Community Groups

Religious Groups

Sports Groups

YOU

Special Talents (art, dance, music, theater, etc.)

Other

DATING AND MARRIAGE

- **Qualities of a Mate**

- **Teen Marriage**

THE "PERFECT" MATE (RC-22)

DIRECTIONS: In the space below, write down all the qualities of a "perfect" mate for you. Then go back over the list and write the codes that apply in the blank to the left.

QUALITIES OF MY "PERFECT" MATE:

_____ 1.

_____ 2.

_____ 3.

_____ 4.

_____ 5.

_____ 6.

_____ 7.

_____ 8.

_____ 9.

_____ 10.

_____ 11.

_____ 12.

_____ 13.

_____ 14.

_____ 15.

_____ 16.

_____ 17.

_____ 18.

_____ 19.

_____ 20.

CODES:

D Your dad has this quality.
M Your mom has this quality
+ You have this quality.
− You wish you had this quality.
B You think both partners need this quality to be happy.
* These are the three most important qualities.

WHERE DO YOU RANK? (RC-23)

DIRECTIONS: Rank each statement from 1 to 3 with one being the best choice and 3 being the worst choice.

1. Which would be hardest for you to accept?
   _____ Your husband or wife cheating on you.
   _____ Your husband or wife becoming dependent on "hard" drugs.
   _____ Finding out your husband or wife was married before, but never told you.

2. What do you look for in a mate?
   _____ someone who is good-looking
   _____ someone who has a lot of money
   _____ someone who is fun to be with

3. What do you look at first when you see someone of the opposite sex?
   _____ their eyes
   _____ their overall figure
   _____ their face

4. Which one of these would you most want to avoid in a relationship?
   _____ boredom
   _____ no communication
   _____ little intimacy

5. Which of these is most preferable to you?
   _____ staying single
   _____ getting married but no kids
   _____ getting married and having kids

6. How would you prefer to meet someone?
   _____ in class
   _____ on a blind date
   _____ at the mall

7. Which best describes you?
   _____ don't like public displays of affection
   _____ hugging is OK in public
   _____ hugging and kissing are OK in public

Name _____ **Date** _____

I AGREE! (RC-24)

DIRECTIONS: Look at the statements below concerning marriage and place an asterisk (*) next to the statements you can most agree with.

_____ 1. Love is all that is necessary in a good marriage.

_____ 2. Love means you never have to say you're sorry.

_____ 3. The male is the head of the household.

_____ 4. A marriage without children is incomplete.

_____ 5. Two people can marry and not love each other.

_____ 6. Love and sex are different.

_____ 7. Jealousy in marriage can be a positive emotion.

_____ 8. It is wrong to have sex unless you are married.

_____ 9. A woman's place is in the kitchen.

_____ 10. It is possible to be in love with two people at once.

_____ 11. Two people must enjoy the same things to stay married.

_____ 12. Divorce is failure.

_____ 13. I would not forgive my spouse for adultery.

_____ 14. People cannot be single and happy.

_____ 15. I would never live with someone outside of marriage.

Name _____ Date _____

I WOULD NEVER DO THAT! (RC-25)

DIRECTIONS: Listed below is a chart that outlines various roles in a marriage. Place a check in the box that most applies to your feelings about each role.

Role	I would definitely do this	I might do this	Not sure if I'd do this	I doubt if I'd do this	I'd never do this
Earn most of the money					
Cook and clean					
Stay home with the kids					
Take care of the car					
Pay the bills					
Do the grocery shopping					
Change the baby's diapers					
Be the family boss					
Take care of the kids while my wife or husband goes on a trip					
Go on a trip alone					
Do the laundry					
Take out the trash					
Take care of a pet					
Discipline the children					

ACTIVITY 7: VOTE FOR ME!

Concept/ Description: Students will vote *yes, no,* or *undecided* on a variety of topics dealing with relationships.

Objective: To generate discussions about relationships.

Materials: Voting Topics sheet (RC-26)

Directions:
1. Read the questions from the Voting Topics sheet one by one.
2. Have students vote <u>yes</u> by raising one hand thumbs up, vote <u>no</u> by raising one hand thumbs down, and vote <u>undecided</u> by folding both arms across the chest.
3. When finished, pick a few topics and discuss. Try to choose the topics that generated the most varied responses.

VOTING TOPICS (RC-26)

1. Do you like kissing or hugging scenes on TV shows or in the movies?

2. Would you watch an X-rated movie?

3. Do you want to marry a virgin?

4. Do you think it's okay for a first-grader to have a boyfriend/girlfriend?

5. Do you think that marriage should last forever?

6. Do you think it's okay to have more than one boyfriend/girlfriend at a time?

7. Would you go on a blind date?

8. Do you think it's okay for a girl to ask out a guy?

9. Do you know of at least one "perfect" marriage?

10. Do you think people should avoid divorce for the sake of the children?

11. Will you have at least two children?

12. Do you think married couples should not display affection in public?

13. Do you think kissing should not be permitted in school?

14. Do you think men think about sex all of the time?

15. Do you think women think about sex just as much as men do?

16. Do you know someone younger than thirteen who has had intercourse?

17. Do you know someone who has had unprotected intercourse?

18. Do you think wives should not work if they don't have to?

19. Do you think mothers should not work while their children are young?

20. Do you think there is a difference between "making love" and "having sex"?

ACTIVITY 8: BATTLE OF THE SEXES

Concept/
Description: Students will discuss what they like and dislike about the opposite sex.

Objective: To allow students to practice good communication skills while discussing what they like and dislike about the opposite sex.

Materials: None

Directions:
1. Have the girls sit in a circle in the center of the room.
2. The boys will form an outer circle.
3. Girls will have approximately 5 to 10 minutes to discuss what they like and dislike about boys. The boys may not speak, comment, or interfere with the girls' discussion in any way. They must sit quietly and wait for their turn.
4. Then, allow the boys to sit in the center with the girls forming the outer circle.
5. The boys will have approximately 5 to 10 minutes to discuss what they like and dislike about girls.
6. After each group has had a turn, discuss ways that the sexes can learn to accept each other. Discuss the role of good communication in relationships.

Name _____ **Date** _____

STEADY READY? (RC-27)

DIRECTIONS: List all of the advantages and disadvantages you can think of in having a steady boyfriend or girlfriend. Discuss your answers with the class.

➕ ADVANTAGES	➖ DISADVANTAGES

ACTIVITY 9: WEDDING SONG

Concept/
Description: Students will pick a wedding song based on their feelings about love and marriage.

Objective: To discuss love and communication in a successful marriage after listening to some of the songs students have chosen for their "wedding songs."

Materials: Songs chosen by students to represent their feelings about love and marriage
CD or tape player

Directions:
1. Have students choose a "wedding song" based on their personal feelings about love and marriage.
2. Students should photocopy the words to the song or write them on a piece of paper and bring it to class.
3. If possible, students should bring the tape, CD, or record to class as well.
4. Choose a few songs to play and discuss. Ask the student who chose the particular song, what meaning it has for him or her.
5. Discuss the importance of love and communication in marriage.

Variations:
1. Have students ask someone who has been married for a long period of time to tell them what he or she believes is the key to a successful marriage. Write down that person's responses.
2. Have students find out what their parents' or grandparents' wedding songs were. If possible, bring some of the songs to class.
3. Invite a couple (perhaps someone's grandparents), who has been married for over 30 years, to class to discuss the key to a successful marriage.

ACTIVITY 10: CAN WE MAKE ENDS MEET?

Concept/ Description: Being a teenage parent can drastically change a person's life socially, emotionally, physically, and financially.

Objective: To explore the financial strain that being a teenage parent would cause the typical teenager.

Materials: Classified section of the newspaper
Teenage Parents sheet (RC-28)
Teenage Parents (2) sheet (RC-29)
Pens or pencils

Directions:
1. Divide the class into groups of four and give each group the Teenage Parents sheets.
2. Ask each group to choose a job from the classified section for which they would be qualified. Assuming that they got the job, estimate how much money they would make in a year. (Call the company, if possible.)
3. Give students a few days to research the information on the sheets by asking people, calling various companies to get rates, etc.
4. Fill in the sheets and figure out if your "income" could cover your "expenses."
5. Ask students to list the many difficulties teenage parents face, besides financial strain.
6. Discuss.

TEENAGE PARENTS (RC-28)

DIRECTIONS: Being a teenage parent can drastically change your life. Figure out the financial aspect of being a teenage parent by filling in the information below:

HOUSING

1. Rent $ _____ per month

2. Utilities

   Gas $ _____ per month
   Electricity $ _____ per month
   Garbage $ _____ per month
   Water $ _____ per month
   Sewer $ _____ per month

3. Approximate phone bill $ _____ per month

4. Cable television $ _____ per month

   TOTAL $ _____ PER MONTH

AUTO

1. Car payment $ _____ per month

2. Gasoline $ _____ per month

3. Car repairs $ _____ per month

4. License and insurance $ _____ per month

   TOTAL $ _____ PER MONTH

BABY

1. Day care $ _____ per month

2. Diapers $ _____ per month

3. Baby clothing $ _____ per month

   TOTAL $ _____ PER MONTH

©1993 by The Center for Applied Research in Education

TEENAGE PARENTS (2) (RC-29)

**G
E
N
E
R
A
L**

1. **Food bill** $ _____ per month

2. **Health care** $ _____ per month

3. **Entertainment** $ _____ per month

4. **Savings** $ _____ per month

5. **Miscellaneous (gifts, toys, etc.)**

                                    TOTAL $ _____ **PER MONTH**

TOTALS:

                    Housing $_____

                    Auto $_____

                    Baby $_____

                    General $_____

TOTAL MONTHLY COSTS $_____

**Do you think that a typical teenager could make ends meet?
Why or why not?**

GENERAL ACTIVITIES-RELATIONSHIPS

ACTIVITY 11: SING IT AGAIN, SAM!

**Concept/
Description:** Students will analyze songs dealing with relationships.

Objective: To listen to and analyze songs dealing with relationships.

Materials: Tapes or CDs about relationships (see suggestions below)
(Note: Students may be willing to bring in or suggest appropriate songs. Be sure to screen them first.)
Portable stereo
Reproduced sheets with the words to the chosen songs
What's It All About? sheet (RC-30)
Pens or pencils
Some song suggestions:
"I Don't Wanna Cry" by Mariah Carey
"Friends" by Elton John
"The Last Song" by Elton John
"The Living Years" by Mike and the Mechanics
"I Hate Everything About You" by Ugly Kid Joe
Most songs by Chicago

Directions: 1. Hand out the What's It All About? sheets and the words to the songs you or the class has chosen.

2. Play a song and have the students read the words as the music is playing.

3. Analyze the songs in groups, or individually, by filling out the What's It All About? sheet.

4. Discuss how music is used to express feelings about relationships.

WHAT'S IT ALL ABOUT? (RC-30)

DIRECTIONS: Listen to the songs about relationships and answer the questions for each.

Song Title:_____ **Artist:**_____

What is the message you get from this song?

Do you think this song sends a positive or negative message about relationships? Why?

Have you ever felt this way?

Song Title:_____ **Artist:**_____

What is the message you get from this song?

Do you think this song sends a positive or negative message about relationships? Why?

Have you ever felt this way?

SKILLS AND METHODS OF COMMUNICATION

- **Ice Breakers**

- **Guidelines for Good Communication**

- **Body Language**

- **Listening Skills**

- **Assertiveness**

- **Speaking Skills**

ACTIVITY 12: NAME CALLING

Concept/ Description: This activity is an ice breaker designed to get to know class members.

Objective: To attempt to remember each class member's name and something about him or her.

Materials: None

Directions:
1. Divide the class into two (or more) large circles.
2. Starting with a volunteer and moving clockwise, have one person introduce themselves, then say one thing they enjoy doing. For example, "My name is Pat and I play lacrosse."
3. The next person would repeat what Pat said, then add his or her own introduction.
4. Allow group members to help if someone starts to struggle with remembering names.
5. Continue until all class members have been introduced.

"Uh... my name is Susie... uh, I mean I'm Bob and she's Susie... and Susie likes rock climbing... er, no... Jim likes rock climbing... or is it Tom?"

ACTIVITY 13: CLASS PICTURES

**Concept/
Description:** In groups, one member will draw pictures while the other group members try to guess a key word or phrase.

Objective: To be the first group to guess the key word or phrase.

Materials: Draw This cards (RC-31–32)
Paper
Pens or pencils
Chalkboard
Chalk

Directions:
1. Divide the class into groups of five or six and give each group some scrap paper. Each group needs pens or pencils.
2. Each member of the group counts off.
3. The teacher sits in the center of the room and when ready, asks all the students numbered one to come look at one of the Draw This cards.
4. Students then quickly return to their seats and begin drawing clues so the group members can guess the word or phrase that was on the teacher's card. Note: No words, letters or numbers may be drawn. No talking is permitted by the person drawing.
5. Group members try to guess what the picture is. They call out their guesses until one is correct or until another group guesses first.
6. The first group to get the correct answer is the winner of the round, and that group receives one point.
7. Keep score on the chalkboard.
8. Continue playing by calling up student two, then three, and so on until everyone has had a chance to draw.
9. The team with the most points is the winner.

"Can't you tell what this is?"

DRAW THIS Cards (RC-31)

a wedding	**shopping**
kissing	**going to the movies**
an argument	**fast food**
a baby crying	**talking on the phone**
a person listening	**arguing with parents**
a fistfight	**best friends**

DRAW THIS Cards (Make Your Own) (RC-32)

ACTIVITY 14: COMMUNICATION GUIDELINES

Concept/ Description: Two transparencies are provided for explaining good and bad communication.

Objective: To discuss what makes good communication and what makes poor communication.

Materials: Communication Dos (RC-33)
Communication Don'ts (RC-34)
Overhead projector
Screen

Directions:
1. Have Communication Dos and Communication Don'ts made into overhead transparencies or write the rules on a large poster.
2. Review the skills needed for good communication and have students give examples.
3. Go over what constitutes poor communication and have students give examples, without naming specific people.
4. Discuss the need for good communication in school, in relationships, on the job, etc.

LISTEN

LOOK THE PERSON IN THE EYES

ASK QUESTIONS

HEAR A PERSON OUT

RESIST DISTRACTIONS

BE OPEN-MINDED

**ASSUME RESPONSIBILITY FOR
A TWO-WAY DIALOGUE**

INTERRUPT

RAISE YOUR VOICE OR YELL

CALL NAMES OR LABEL

BLAME

FORCE OR THREATEN

LAUGH AT PEOPLE

ASSUME YOU UNDERSTAND

MAKE SNAP JUDGMENTS

SAY "ALWAYS" OR "NEVER"

OFFER ADVICE WHEN IT'S NOT ASKED FOR

ACTIVITY 15: BODY LANGUAGE MATCH GAME

Concept/ Description: Body language can often indicate how a person is feeling or what he or she is thinking.

Objective: Students will try to match pictures of body language with terms describing it

Materials: Body Language Match Game cards (RC-35–36)
Flat surface (desk, table or floor)

Directions: 1. Divide the class into groups of three or four and give each group a set of Match Game cards.

2. Place the cards face down on the table.

3. One at a time, players turn over two game cards. If the picture matches with the correct term describing the picture, it is considered a match and that player takes both cards. If it is a match, the player gets another turn. If it is not a match, both cards are turned face down and the next player goes.

4. Play continues until all cards have been matched.

5. The player with the most cards is the winner.

BODY LANGUAGE Match Game Cards (RC-35)

BODY LANGUAGE Match Game Cards (RC-36)

ECSTATIC	**CONFUSED**	**SAD**
DISGUSTED	**IN LOVE**	**ANGRY**
AFRAID OR NERVOUS	**HAPPY**	**EXHAUSTED**

Name _____   Date _____

KINESICS (RC-37)

DIRECTIONS: Kinesics is the science of body language. It is a way of communicating mood, attitude, or information through body movements, posture, gestures, and facial expressions. Body language can send a message while a person is speaking, or it can send a silent message of its own. Read each example and write down what you think the body language is indicating.

Your sister, head lowered, shoulders slumped, drags herself off the basketball court after her team's last-second defeat in the playoffs. What does her body language indicate?

Your teacher rolls his eyes, places his hand firmly on his hips, taps his foot, then fold his arms and waits because the class is disruptive. What does his body language say?

Your mother quickly glares in your direction, wrinkles her forehead, and frowns when you tell an inappropriate joke at a family gathering. What does her body language indicate?

While talking to a friend, he looks around, shifts his position constantly, and taps his fingers. What does his body language tell you?

While the teacher is talking, you slouch in your seat, yawn, and look at your watch. What does your body language indicate?

Name _____   Date _____

TOON IN TO BODY LANGUAGE (RC-38)

DIRECTIONS: Shown below are some cartoons without the dialogue. Look at each one and imagine what each is saying, then write the dialogue in the bubbles.

ACTIVITY 16: CLASS CHARADES

**Concept/
Description:** Students must use only expressions and body language to convey a message.

Objective: To be the first group to successfully identify each message.

Materials: Class Charades cards (RC-39)

Directions:
1. Divide the class into two groups.
2. Place a set of Class Charades cards, face down, in front of each group.
3. On the teacher's signal, one group member picks up a card and acts out the message written on the card. The actor may not talk or write.
4. The group members call out their guesses until the exact message or word is called out. The next player then picks a card and acts out that message.
5. Play proceeds until all the cards have been guessed by one team.
6. The first team to do this is the winner.
7. Discuss. Ask students why they think some messages were harder than others to convey without using words.

CLASS CHARADES Cards (RC-39)

MAD AT THE WORLD	**LOST AND FOUND**
SPLITTING HEADACHE	**SCARED TO DEATH**
SWEATING LIKE A PIG	**CRYING LIKE A BABY**
SICK AND TIRED	**JUMPING FOR JOY**

LISTEN TO ME! (RC-40)

DIRECTIONS: How much time do you spend listening during a typical school day? Look at the pie chart below and answer the questions.

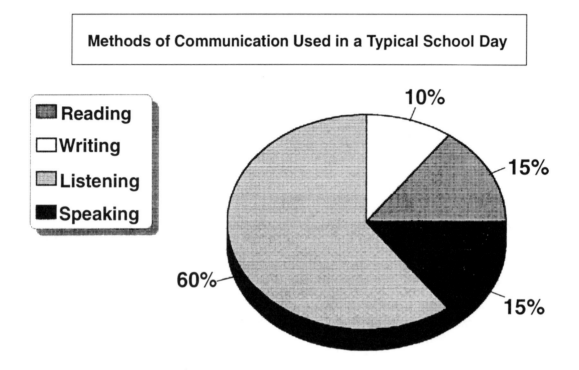

Methods of Communication Used in a Typical School Day

Reading
Writing
Listening
Speaking

10%

15%

60%

15%

1. According to the pie chart, approximately what percentage of the school day is spent listening?

2. Why do you think this is the case?

3. Based on this graph, why is it important to have good listening skills?

4. What types of problems can result from not listening well? Explain.

5. Give a specific example of a time you did not listen well in school.

ACTIVITY 17: PEANUT BUTTER AND JELLY?

Concept/ Description: Listening skills are required for good communication.

Objective: To give clear directions for a simple task and have a volunteer attempt to follow the directions to the letter.

Materials: Jar of peanut butter
Jar of jelly
Loaf of bread in the wrapper
Butter knife and spoon
Napkin
Paper plate

Directions: 1. Place the above items on a desk for all to see.

2. Ask students to write down all the steps for making a peanut butter and jelly sandwich. Tell them to be specific and assume nothing.

3. Ask a volunteer to read the directions that he or she has written, while you attempt to make the sandwich as stated. Don't assume anything. If they tell you to place the jelly on the bread, did they mention that you had to open the jar first? If not, simply place the jar of jelly on the loaf of bread.

4. After each unsuccessful attempt, allow the group to try to add to the details of their directions until the sandwich is made correctly.

5. Although this is a silly example of giving and following directions, ask students when not understanding or giving clear directions could be dangerous or cause a problem.

6. Discuss.

ACTIVITY 18: DILEMMA

Concept/
Description: To give each member of a group a chance to voice their opinion on topics related to dating.

Objective: To choose a card and give your uninterrupted opinion on the dilemma presented.

Materials: Dilemma cards (RC-41)

Directions:
1. Divide the class into groups of four and give each group a set of Dilemma cards.
2. Each person chooses a card and, in turn, reads it aloud.
3. Each person gets to give an uninterrupted opinion before the rest of the group may join in the discussion.
4. After all the topics have been discussed, discuss a few of the topics as a class.
5. Ask students how it felt to give an uninterrupted opinion. Ask if they get to do that often. Who do they feel interrupts them the most (parents, friends, siblings)?
6. Why is it important that people be allowed to express themselves without interruption? Why do people interrupt? What does that say to the person being interrupted? Discuss.

Hmmmmmm....
What would I do?

DILEMMA Cards (RC-41)

What if your best friend had an STD and asked you not to tell anyone, but then started dating another good friend of yours?	What would you do if your best friend's boyfriend or girlfriend was cheating on him or her?
What would you consider "the perfect date"?	What would you do if your best friend had just broken up with a boyfriend/girlfriend and that former steady now asked you out?
What would you do if you didn't approve of your son's or daughter's boyfriend or girlfriend?	What would you do if you found a condom in your son's back pocket when washing his jeans?
What would you do if you found birth control pills in your daughter's purse while cleaning her room?	What would you do if your date talked to someone else all night while at a party with you?

PASSIVE LISTENING (RC-42)

DIRECTIONS: Passive listening is showing a person that you are interested without really speaking. In the box below, you will find some passive listening techniques. Choose one of the topics for discussion from the Topics for Discussion sheet (RC-44) and, with a partner, have a conversation with one person speaking and the other listening passively. Change roles so that both will get a chance to speak and listen. When finished, answer the questions below the box.

Passive Listening Techniques

Make eye contact.
Nod your head.
Lean forward.
Reflect your feelings with facial expressions.
Use short encouraging verbal responses ("uh-huh").

---

1. When you were the listener, did you find it difficult to remain quiet? Why or why not?

2. Did you have to concentrate on listening passively or did it come naturally?

3. Have you ever spoken to someone who couldn't wait to voice his or her opinion? How could you tell? Describe his or her body language.

4. Did you like speaking with a passive listener? Why or why not?

5. Did your partner appear interested in what you were saying? How did that make you feel?

©1993 by The Center for Applied Research in Education

Name _____ **Date** _____

ACTIVE LISTENING (RC-43)

DIRECTIONS: Active listening is using verbal responses to show acceptance, understanding, respect, sympathy, and encouragement. In the box are some active listening techniques. Choose one of the topics for discussion from the Topics for Discussion sheet (RC-44) and, with a partner, have a conversation with one person speaking and the other listening actively. Change roles so that both will get a chance to speak and listen. When finished, answer the questions below the box.

Active Listening Techniques

Use verbal responses ("Really?," "I see," "What happened next?").
Comment directly on what is being said.
Restate the speaker's ideas in your own words ("Do you mean...?).
Encourage the person to express feelings ("I guess you must have felt...").
Encourage more information ("Tell me about...").
Don't pass judgment.

---

1. When you were the listener, did you find it difficult to use active listening? Why or why not?

2. Did you have to concentrate on active listening or did it come naturally?

3. Have you ever spoken to someone who constantly interrupted you? How did that make you feel?

4. Did you like speaking with an active listener? Why or why not?

5. Did your partner appear genuinely interested in what you were saying or were you aware that he or she was trying to use active listening? Explain.

TOPICS FOR DISCUSSION (RC-44)

1. Describe one of the funniest situations you have ever been in.

2. Tell about the scariest thing that ever happened to you.

3. Tell about the proudest moment in your life.

4. Talk about someone you admire and why.

5. Talk about your favorite actor or actress and why you like him or her.

6. In your opinion, what was the greatest moment in sports?

7. Talk about your best moment in sports.

8. What is your greatest accomplishment?

9. What talents do you possess? Explain.

10. Talk about your favorite vacation.

11. What is the worst time you've ever had on a vacation?

12. If someone gave you $100,000, what would you do with it?

13. What is your greatest fear? Explain.

14. If you could go anywhere in the world, where would you go and why?

15. If you could change one thing about the world, what would you change and why?

Name _____ **Date** _____

ARE YOU ASSERTIVE? (RC-45)

DIRECTIONS: Take the Assertiveness Test below by writing YES or NO in the blank to the left.

_____ 1. I have apologized for something that wasn't my fault.

_____ 2. I have spoken to someone for longer than I wanted to because I didn't want to hurt the person's feeling by cutting him or her off.

_____ 3. I feel uncomfortable or embarrassed if I receive compliments.

_____ 4. I've been angry at someone just because my friends were.

_____ 5. I've been out on a date with someone I didn't want to date because I felt bad about saying no.

_____ 6. I've done something I shouldn't have done because I felt pressured to do it.

_____ 7. I get really upset and hurt if someone is angry with me.

_____ 8. If I received the wrong food at a restaurant, I would have a hard time asking the server to take it back.

_____ 9. I've worn something I didn't really like because others were wearing it.

_____ 10. I've gone someplace I didn't want to go because I didn't want to start an argument.

Did you answer yes to any questions? Most people have some instances where they are not as assertive as they would like to be. How could you become more assertive?

PASSIVE, AGGRESSIVE, OR ASSERTIVE? (RC-46)

DIRECTIONS: Write *aggressive, assertive,* or *passive* in the blank to the left to describe the response to each question.

_____ 1. Can you help me with my book report? I won't get a chance to read the whole book.

   Why should I help you? You're too lazy! It's not my problem!

_____ 2. Can I borrow your new outfit? I won't ruin it.

   Well...I didn't get a chance to wear it yet, but...well, okay.

_____ 3. I need to borrow $50 to pay a traffic ticket. How 'bout lending it to me?

   I'm really not able to lend you the money. I can't help you out.

_____ 4. Let's go to the mall and hang out tonight. There's nothing better to do.

   I don't want to go to the mall tonight. I'd prefer to go to the movies.

_____ 5. Can I be on your team for basketball?

   No! You stink...besides, we have enough players already!

_____ 6. Let's have a few beers—no one is home and they'll never find out.

   I'm not sure if that's such a good idea...but, okay, I guess it would be allright.

_____ 7. Let's skip school and go to the beach today.

   I'm not taking a chance like that. I'm going to school.

_____ 8. Can I stay at your house for the weekend?

   Well...I was having a friend from my old neighborhood stay over, but okay...I guess so.

_____ 9. Give me your homework to copy...I was on the phone all night.

   No, do your own work, you idiot!

_____ 10. Can you babysit for me this weekend?

   I made other plans with my friends. I won't be able to help you this particular weekend.

©1993 by The Center for Applied Research in Education

Call me Einstein but...
I'd say this is AGGRESSIVE!!

Name _____ **Date** _____

TAKING CHARGE (RC-47)

DIRECTIONS: For each situation, write one passive, one aggressive, and one assertive response. One example has been done for you.

You are at a friend's house and you would like something to drink.
Aggressive: "Get me a drink."
Passive: Sit quietly and never ask for a drink.
Assertive: "I'm very thirsty. Would you mind if I had a glass of water?"

You have been waiting in line a long time at an amusement park and a woman with three kids tries to push ahead of you.

Aggressive: _____

Passive: _____

Assertive: _____

Your mother buys you a sweater that you really dislike.

Aggressive: _____

Passive: _____

Assertive: _____

Your boyfriend or girlfriend wants you to go to a rock concert to hear a group you really don't want to hear.

Aggressive: _____

Passive: _____

Assertive: _____

A person you have met before starts gossiping viciously about your best friend.

Aggressive: _____

Passive: _____

Assertive: _____

Your circle of friends wants to have a party at your house while your parents are away.

Aggressive: _____

Passive: _____

Assertive: _____

Name _____ **Date** _____

DOOR OPENERS (RC-48)

DIRECTIONS: Door openers are statements that keep a conversation going and encourage the other person to speak. Listed below are some examples of door openers:

Tell me more!
That's a good idea.
What happened next?
And then what did you do?
What do you think about...?
Really?
I'd like to know more about that!
Do you have any suggestions?

Write a conversation between two friends that uses door openers. Write the conversation below:

©1993 by The Center for Applied Research in Education

74

Name _____ **Date** _____

NO MEANS NO! (RC-49)

DIRECTIONS: Review the steps to saying no and still remaining friends. Then, with a partner, try role playing the situations in the box. Consider this point: If a friend doesn't accept <u>no</u> as an answer, is he/she really a friend?

NO

HOW TO SAY NO:

1. **Decide how you feel ahead of time** so you won't be caught off guard. This will give you confidence and control over your choices.
2. **Be friendly, but be firm.** Repeat what your friend said. (You want me to cut school and drink all day?)
3. **Be honest.** Don't lie or you may be forced to make up more lies to cover the first one. Simply state the truth. (I really don't want to do that.)
4. **Speak only for yourself.** You're not responsible for everyone else's actions. Speak only about how you feel.
5. **Discuss the possible consequences.** (If I were to get caught drinking, I'd be grounded and it's not worth it.)
6. **Separate the activity from the person.** Let them know you care about them, but you do not wish to do what they want. (You're a great friend, but I don't feel comfortable drinking and cutting school.)
7. **Suggest an alternative.** (Let's plan to go to the shore this weekend instead.)
8. **If the person persists, walk away from the situation.** Suggest that they join you in something else. (I'm going to school now. I'll be at the usual table at lunch, and I hope you'll meet me there.)
9. **Be prepared to accept the fact that you may be rejected anyway.**

NO

NO

ROLE PLAY SITUATIONS:

Jane wants to cut school and go to the mall all day, but Sue has a major test that she cannot afford to miss.

Rob is sure he can shoplift some CDs without getting caught and wants Mike to help. Mike doesn't want to get in any trouble and feels very uncomfortable about the situation.

Leanne wants Bill to smoke pot with her, but Bill really doesn't want to get involved with drugs in any way. He really likes Leanne and has wanted to ask her out for a long time.

Jim sees an opportunity to steal the teacher's roll book and asks Ryan to hide it in his desk until the end of the period. Ryan doesn't want to get caught with the roll book.

Len wants Kristen to go farther than she is ready to go. He threatens to break up with her if she doesn't sleep with him soon.

NO

Name _____ **Date** _____

"I" STATEMENTS (RC-50)

DIRECTIONS: An "I" statement is a statement of your feelings that does not blame or judge the other person. The statement starts with "I feel...," "I want...," "I'm upset because..." Change the "You" statements below into "I" statements.

"You" Statements	"I" Statements
You never call me when I ask you to!	I wish we could talk on the phone more often.
Will you turn down your stereo? I can't hear myself think!	
Will you clean your room? I've asked you to do it five times!	
You are so annoying when you tease me!	
Why don't you grow up and stop acting like a baby?!	
Will you stop interrupting me?	
You're such a loud mouth!	
You can't play basketball, you stink! Go play on another team.	
It's your fault I got in trouble! Why did you have to tell on me?	
You never listen when I give you directions!	
You always ignore me when your other friends are around!	
You never let me do anything!	
Why don't you do your own homework and stop copying mine?!	
You are so moody sometimes!	
You never told us the assignment was due today! That's not fair!	

GROUP DYNAMICS

- Cooperation

- Brainstorming

- Compromise

ACTIVITY 19: COOPERATION PUZZLE

Concept/
Description: Students will cooperate in an attempt to put puzzles together without talking.

Objective: For four students to put five puzzles together without using
verbal communication.

Materials: Cooperation Puzzles (have five puzzles for every group of four)
(RC-51)
Flat surface, such as a desk, table, or floor
Envelopes (one per student)

Directions: 1. Divide the class into groups of no more than four students.

2. Prior to class, take a set of five puzzles and mix up the pieces.
Take four envelopes and randomly place the pieces in the
four envelopes. Be sure not to mix up the sets of 5. (Color
coding each set of five prevents a mix-up.)

3. Give each group a set of envelopes containing puzzle pieces
for five puzzles.

4. Have each student open his or her envelope, remove the
pieces, and place them on the floor or other flat surface.

5. Without talking, writing, etc., each group is to try to put
together five squares.

6. No player may take a puzzle piece from another player; that
player must give the piece needed.

7. When one group has completed all five puzzles, have all
groups stop.

8. Discuss problems or frustrations the groups encountered.
Was it aggravating seeing a piece that you needed, but
having to wait until the person gave it to you? Would talking
have made the task easier?

COOPERATION PUZZLE PIECES (RC-51)

DIRECTIONS: Trace the puzzle pieces onto oaktag or cardboard. Laminate and then carefully cut out the pieces and place them in an envelope. You will need five puzzles for every group of four students. It may be helpful to use different colored paper for each set so as not to mix them.

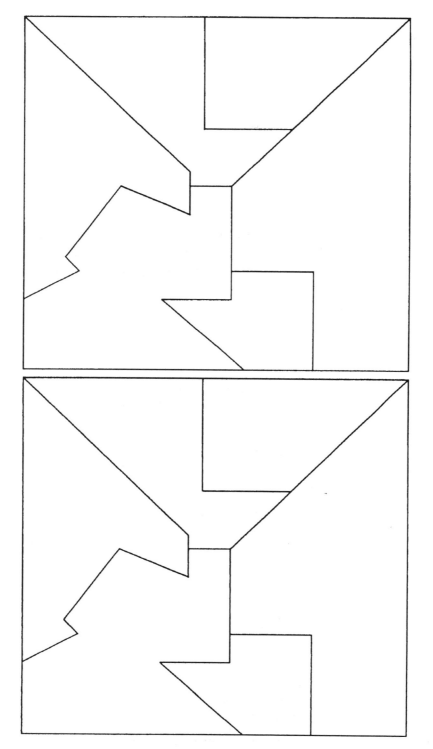

ACTIVITY 20: BUILD A BETTER MOUSETRAP

Concept/ Description: To examine group dynamics while carrying out a cooperative task.

Objective: To be the group to build the highest tower with the materials given.

Materials: Group Dynamics sheet (RC-52)
Construction paper
Scissors
Masking tape
Glue

Directions:

1. Divide the class into groups of five and give each group the same amount of materials.

2. Tell the students they will have about 10 minutes to build the highest self-supporting structure they can. (In other words, the tower cannot be attached to the walls, desks, etc., and must start from the floor.)

3. While the groups are being timed, the teacher writes down observations about the dynamics of each group to later share with the groups.

4. When the time limit is up, stop the groups, and hand out the Group Dynamics sheet for each group to complete.

5. Discuss how the groups functioned and whether the activity automatically became competitive among the groups. (The teacher never said it was a competition, but did the class assume it was? If so, why?)

6. The teacher then shares his or her observations.

GROUP DYNAMICS (RC-52)

DIRECTIONS: Now that your group has completed the activity, answer the questions and discuss how your group functioned.

1. Who became the leader in your group?

2. How was the leadership decided?

3. Were there any disagreements? If so, why?

4. Did all members of your group get a chance to give ideas or suggestions?

5. Were anyone's ideas blocked or put down?

6. Did everyone actively participate in building?

7. How well do you think your group functioned? Explain.

Comments:

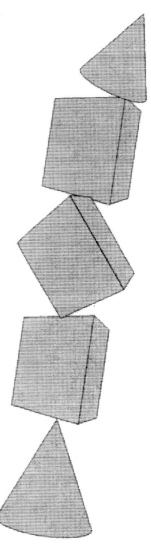

BRAINSTORM (RC-53)

DIRECTIONS: Cooperation is working together towards a common goal. Brainstorming requires cooperation and the ability to follow clearly defined guidelines. In groups of four, try brainstorming a solution to one of the problems listed below. Follow the brainstorming guidelines listed in the box.

BRAINSTORMING GUIDELINES:

1. Your group has 5 minutes to come up with as many solutions as possible.
2. Write down *every* idea. Have one group member record them.
3. *Do not* pass judgment (good or bad) on any of the ideas; just record them.
4. Go for the unusual ideas as well as the usual. Sometimes the wildest ones can turn out to be the best.
5. Try to get as many ideas as possible in the given time period.

BRAINSTORMING TOPICS:

1. Where should we go on the class trip this year?

2. What should be done about smoking in school?

3. What can be done to improve the food in the cafeteria?

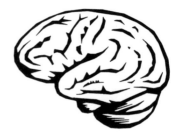

4. What can our school do to raise money for the homeless?

5. What other activities should the school sponsor?

6. What should we have as the prom theme this year?

7. What would you change about this school if you could?

8. What could be done to lessen stealing in the locker rooms?

©1993 by The Center for Applied Research in Education

COMPROMISE (RC-54)

DIRECTIONS: Compromising is giving up something in order to reach an agreement. It is a process of giving and taking to agree on a common goal. Using the situations listed, first brainstorm the solutions, then compromise on the final decision. The guidelines for compromising are listed below:

COMPROMISE GUIDELINES:

1. Everyone *must* get a chance to voice an opinion.
2. All group members have a say in the final decision.
3. Any decision must be approved by *everyone* in the group.
4. *Everyone* must agree to support the final decision.

COMPROMISE TOPICS:

1. If you could invite any famous person to your school for one day, who should be invited?

2. A gift of $200,000 was given to your school by a wealthy graduate. How should the money be spent?

3. The school has decided to give your group an all-expenses paid trip to anywhere in the world for one week. Where will you go?

COMMUNICATION BREAKDOWN

- **Mixed Messages**

- **Eye Contact**

- **Poor Communication**

- **Conflict Resolution**

SPLITTING HEADACHE (RC-55)

DIRECTIONS: Sometimes adults practice "split-level" communication. They disguise messages by saying one thing but meaning something else. For example, some parents may say "yes" in a way that it's difficult to tell if they mean "no," "maybe," or "I don't care." Look at the mixed messages below and write what you think is really being said.

1. Jaime wants to go to a party with her boyfriend. Her father says in a sarcastic voice, "Go right ahead, don't let me spoil your fun!"

_____

_____

_____

2. Your mother says, "Go out and enjoy yourself. I'll stay here all day and do your laundry."

_____

_____

_____

3. Finances have been a little tight and you need $10 to go out on a date. Your mom says, "Help yourself. We have plenty of money to spend on the movies."

_____

_____

_____

4. On your way out the door your mom says, "I expect you home exactly at midnight." Your dad, however, winks at you and says, "Don't be late."

_____

_____

_____

5. While looking at college applications, your parents continually remark about how wonderful the college your dad attended is. Both parents say, "Well, whatever you decide, we're sure you'll make the right choice. We just want you to be happy."

_____

_____

_____

ACTIVITY 21: CONTACT

Concept/ Description: Eye contact is essential to good communication.

Objective: To show the importance of eye contact in good communication.

Materials: Contact Paper (RC-56)
Pens or pencils

Directions:
1. Have students work in pairs and give each student a Contact Paper.
2. Ask students to have a 30- to 45-second conversation in the following manner:
   a. One partner stands, the other sits in a chair.
   b. Both stand, facing each other only a few inches apart.
   c. Both stand with one partner facing the opposite direction.
   d. Both partners stand back to back.
   e. Both sit back to back about 5 feet apart.
   f. One partner talks while the other looks around the room but not at the person talking.
   g. Both talk at the same time but do not look at each other.
3. Each time have students talk about a different subject. Some examples are:
   a. a time you were scared
   b. your favorite vacation spot
   c. the worst food you've ever eaten
   d. your relationship with a brother or sister
   e. something you'd change about the school if you could
   f. the most boring job to have
4. The teacher times the conversations and allows a minute or two in between each conversation so students can fill out the Contact Paper.
5. When pairs have tried each type of conversation, discuss the experience as a class. Ask students which type of conversation bothered them the most and why? Ask if they've ever tried to talk to someone who wasn't looking at them. How did this make them feel?
6. Stress the importance of making eye contact in job interviews, public speaking, general conversation, etc.

CONTACT PAPER (RC-56)

DIRECTIONS: Hold a 30- to 45-second conversation with a partner in the manner shown below. Your teacher will give you the topic each time. Then, after talking in the manner described, write down how you felt about each experience. Which method of talking was the most difficult?

Conversation 1: One partner stands, the other sits in a chair.
How did you feel about talking in this manner?

Conversation 2: Both partners stand facing each other a few inches apart.
How did you feel about talking in this manner?

Conversation 3: Both partners stand, one partner turns and faces the opposite direction.
How did you feel about talking in this manner?

Conversation 4: Both partners stand back to back.
How did you feel about talking in this manner?

Conversation 5: Both partners sit back to back about 5 feet apart.
How did you feel about talking in this manner?

Conversation 6: One partner talks while the other looks around the room but not at the person talking.
How did you feel about talking in this manner?

Conversation 7: Both talk at the same time but do not make eye contact.
How did you feel about talking in this manner?

ACTIVITY 22: I'VE GOT A SECRET

Concept/
Description: There are many things that can interfere with good communication.

Objective: To whisper a secret from person to person and determine what can cause the message to break down.

Materials: I've Got a Secret worksheet (RC-57)
Pens or pencils

Directions: 1. Give each student an I've Got a Secret worksheet, then choose a "secret" from the list below, or make up your own sensible or nonsense secret.

2. Tell the class that you will whisper a "secret" to the first person who, in turn, will whisper it to the next person, and so on, until the "secret" has reached the last person. *Students may not ask questions or repeat a message.*

3. After each student has passed on the message, he or she will fill out the worksheet.

4. When the message has been passed, compare the first and last "secrets." Were students able to relay the correct message, or has much of the content been lost?

5. Have each person read the "secret" written on their papers to determine where the line of communication broke down.

6. Discuss what interferes with good communication.

LIST OF "SECRETS":

1. Three men carried four potatoes, a watermelon, a quilt, and two timepieces into the temple.

2. In 1981, John Hinkley, Jr. shot President Reagan and two other men and was declared not guilty by reason of insanity.

3. A good way to avoid stress is to avoid stressful situations that are not necessary and to take advantage of personal time to do things you enjoy.

4. I once knew a man who went skydiving, surfing, and skin-diving after eating twenty pancakes for breakfast.

5. We went to the zoo to see the camels, hippos, monkeys, and chimpanzees, but instead we only saw a porcupine.

I'VE GOT A SECRET (RC-57)

DIRECTIONS: After you pass the "secret" on to the next person, fill out this sheet.

1. Write down exactly what you heard:

2. Place a check next to all of the things that interfered with you getting the message:

   _____ The speaker spoke too softly.
   _____ The speaker spoke too fast.
   _____ The speaker mumbled.
   _____ I wasn't ready.
   _____ The room was too noisy.
   _____ I wasn't concentrating.
   _____ I misunderstood the directions.
   _____ I wasn't in the mood to do this activity.
   _____ I didn't get it because it didn't make sense.
   _____ Other reason(s):

3. Put a check next to all of the things that prevented you from accurately giving the message:

   _____ It didn't make sense, so I changed it.
   _____ I wasn't sure what was said, so I guessed.
   _____ I mumbled.
   _____ I spoke too fast.
   _____ I spoke too softly.
   _____ The listener wasn't really paying attention.
   _____ Other reason(s):

ACTIVITY 23: BUTT OUT!

**Concept/
Description:** Interrupting and changing the subject are two factors that interfere with good communication.

Objective: To demonstrate how frustrating interruptions can be.

Materials: Butt Out! sheet (RC-58)
Pens or pencils

Directions:
1. Divide the class into partners and give each person a Butt Out! sheet.
2. Have students refer to the Butt Out! sheet and explain that the phrases written are common ways that people interrupt each other.
3. Have one partner start a conversation about anything. The other partner should constantly interrupt using one of the phrases on the sheet, or any other phrase.
4. Reverse roles. Each person should attempt to talk for a few minutes.
5. Ask students to answer the questions at the bottom of the Butt Out! sheet and discuss the frustrations the pairs felt.

"And then I said..."   **"That's nothing...guess what I said?"**

Name _____ **Date** _____

BUTT OUT! (RC-58)

DIRECTIONS: Use the phrases below to interrupt your partner while your partner attempts to speak. You may also use phrases of your own. When finished, answer the questions below.

"Speaking of that…"
"That reminds me…"
"Oh, right, remember the time…"
"That's like the time…"
"That's nothing! Wait'll you hear this…"
"You think that's bad? Let me tell you about…"
"Wait! This is worse…"
"While I'm thinking of it…"

1. What did you learn from this experience?

2. Have you ever interrupted another person to tell a story of your own? If so, why?

3. What do you think it says to the other person when you interrupt in this manner?

4. If someone kept interrupting you, would you tell him or her about it? Why or why not?

ACTIVITY 24: WILL SOMEBODY PLEASE LISTEN?

Concept/ Description: Good communication involves listening, as well as speaking.

Objective: To illustrate the frustration of talking while no one is listening.

Materials: None

Directions:
1. Divide the class into groups of four to five and have them sit in a circle.
2. Ask one volunteer from each group to give a quick summary of their life from birth to the present when you signal them to do so.
3. Instruct all other group members to completely ignore the speaker. They may talk, look around, close their eyes or do anything *except* leave the circle.
4. The speaker must attempt to get the group to listen to his or her story.
5. After about 2 or 3 minutes, stop the activity and discuss.
6. Allow each volunteer to voice his or her feelings about being ignored.
7. Discuss the importance of listening and the effect non-listening has on the speaker.

No one ever listens to me!!

COMMUNICATION BREAKDOWN (RC-59)

DIRECTIONS: Listed below are some of the things that interfere with good communication and conflict resolution.

GIVING ORDERS

PUT DOWNS

I guess if that's the best you can do...

Clean your room, NOW!!!

PREACHING OR MORALIZING

You should know better. I'd be ashamed of myself.

GIVING UNSOLICITED ADVICE OR SOLUTIONS

RIDICULE

That's a stupid idea...you're an idiot!

This is what you should do...

CRITICISM

Can't you do anything right?

Name _____ Date _____

DOOR SLAMMERS (RC-60)

DIRECTIONS: Door slammers are statements that abruptly end a conversation and are often rude and insensitive. Listed below are some examples of door slammers:

That's stupid!   So...what's your point?
Forget It!   Shut up!
That'll never work!   That's out of the question!
That's crazy!   No way!
Are you serious?   It stinks!
That's ridiculous!   That's nonsense!
Are you out of your mind?   Who cares?
That's insane!   Big deal!
That's pathetic!   That's a dumb idea!

Write out a conversation between two friends concerning where to go on a Friday night. Have both people use door slammers to communicate. Write your conversation below:

ACTIVITY 25: ONE-WAY COMMUNICATION

Concept/Description: One-way communication allows for no questions or clarification and involves one person speaking.

Objective: To show students the difficulties that arise from using one-way communication.

Materials: One-Way Communication Picture cards (RC-61)
Paper
Pens or pencils

Directions:
1. Explain that one-way communication involves one person speaking, but there is no give and take. No questions may be asked and there is no way to clarify statements made. One-way communication leaves a great deal of room for misinterpretation.

2. To demonstrate this, ask for a volunteer to describe a picture for the class to draw. (Choose one of the "pictures" from the One-Way Communication Picture cards.)

3. Tell the class that they may not speak in any way. They cannot ask for something to be repeated, they cannot ask questions, etc.

4. When finished, ask class members to show their pictures. Do any of them come close to the picture the volunteer has on the card? Why is one-way communication an ineffective method of communication? What frustrations did class members experience?

5. Discuss times when students felt they were being "talked at" rather than "talked to." How does it make you feel?

6. Finally, discuss why two-way communication is more effective.

Variation: Repeat the activity using two-way communication and compare the pictures to the original being described. Are these drawings closer to the original? Why?

"Is this close enough?"

ONE-WAY COMMUNICATION PICTURE Cards

ACTIVITY 26: IN A RAGE

Concept/ Description: Anger can be expressed in both destructive and constructive ways.

Objective: To make a bulletin board of magazine or newspaper stories of people who used their anger constructively and people who used their anger destructively.

Materials: Magazine and newspaper articles of people using anger constructively and destructively
Scissors
Construction paper
Staples and stapler

Directions:
1. Have students find articles dealing with people who have used their anger in both constructive and destructive ways.
2. Divide a bulletin board in half and label one side "Anger: Constructive" and the other side "Anger: Destructive."
3. Staple the articles under the proper headings and discuss.
4. What methods did the people who used their anger constructively employ to get things done?
5. How could the people who used their anger destructively have done something constructive instead?
6. How do you handle your own anger? Discuss.

DESTRUCTIVE

CONSTRUCTIVE

ACTIVITY 27: CONFLICTING STORIES

**Concept/
Description:** Students will view a video of a television argument or fight.

Objective: To analyze the way the television conflict was resolved.

Materials: Conflicting Stories Questionnaire (RC-62)
Video of television program showing conflict
TV and VCR
Pens or pencils

Directions: 1. Prior to class, videotape a TV program that shows a conflict.
2. Give each student a Conflicting Stories Questionnaire.
3. Show the video of a conflict.
4. Have students answer the questions on the worksheet, and then discuss the following:
   - Were the people involved in the conflict respectful of each other?
   - How would you solve the conflict?
   - Was the television show a realistic portrayal of the way people handle conflicts? Why or why not?

CONFLICTING STORIES Questionnaire (RC-62)

DIRECTIONS: View the videotape of a conflict and answer the questions below.

1. Who was arguing? (adult, child, male, female, husband, wife, brother, sister, etc.)

2. What was the argument about?

3. Describe what happened during the conflict.

4. Was there a solution? If so, what was the solution?

5. Could you identify with any of the characters? If so, whom? Explain why.

6. How would you have solved this problem?

©1993 by The Center for Applied Research in Education

WANNA FIGHT? (RC-63)

DIRECTIONS: Think of a recent conflict you have had, and answer the questions below.

1. Who was involved in the conflict?

2. What was the disagreement about? (Check one or more.)

_____ I was blamed for something I didn't do.

_____ Someone called me a name.

_____ Someone broke a promise.

_____ I was told to do something I didn't want to do.

_____ Someone ruined something of mine.

_____ Someone was rude to me.

_____ Someone was bothering me.

_____ Other (explain):

3. How did you feel about the argument or conflict?

4. How did you feel about the person with whom you were arguing?

5. How did you express your feelings?

6. How did the other person express his or her feelings?

7. Did you agree on a solution? If so, what was it?

ACTIVITY 28: CONFLICT RESOLUTION

Concept/ Description: Many conflicts can be resolved by staying calm and using the steps in conflict resolution.

Objective: To use the steps in conflict resolution while roleplaying conflict situations.

Materials: Steps to Resolving Conflicts sheet (RC-64)
Conflicts Roleplay sheet (RC-65)

Directions:
1. Hand each student a Steps to Resolving Conflicts sheet.
2. Review the steps with the class.
3. Have the students pair up and give each pair a Conflicts Roleplay sheet.
4. Ask students to roleplay the situations and attempt to resolve the conflicts by using the steps discussed.
5. Discuss.

STEPS TO RESOLVING CONFLICTS (RC-64)

Conflicts can be resolved if the parties involved stay calm and use the following steps:

1. STATE THE PROBLEM

Clearly and calmly state the problem using "I" statements. Don't pass judgment, accuse, or blame the other person.

2. DEFINE THE SCOPE OF THE PROBLEM

Discuss the specific areas in which you agree and disagree.

3. BRAINSTORM POSSIBLE SOLUTIONS

List all the possible solutions that you both can come up with to resolve the conflict. Write down all the ideas even if they seem ridiculous at the time.

4. IDENTIFY CONSEQUENCES

Discuss the possible consequences for each of the brainstormed solutions.

5. CHOOSE A SOLUTION

Choose a solution that you both can agree upon.

CONFLICTS ROLEPLAY (RC-65)

DIRECTIONS: Using the Steps to Resolving Conflicts sheet (RC-64), roleplay the situations listed below with a partner. For each situation, generate ideas for what you could say. Then, determine what solutions are possible.

ROLE PLAYS:

1. Your best friend borrowed a brand new CD from you for a party. When returned, the CD skipped and appeared scratched. You never had a chance to play it before you lent it to your friend.

2. Your sister or brother borrowed an expensive sweatshirt from you. You were planning to wear it to a party this evening. When you got it back, you noticed a grease stain on the sleeve.

3. Your dad has been on the phone for 30 minutes and you need to use the phone to get an important homework assignment. The assignment will take at least an hour and you are already tired.

4. You are waiting to meet a friend at the movies. Your friend arrives 25 minutes late for a movie you really want to see. You have missed the beginning of the movie. This is not the first time your friend has been late.

5. You arrive early at a football game and place your jacket on the bleachers to reserve your seat while you go to look for a friend. When you come back you find your jacket on the ground and a person in your seat.

6. You and a partner have a major social studies project due. Each time you try to meet with your partner, he or she has something else that has to be done. You need to get this project done in order to get a good grade in the class.

7. Your sister is practicing her tuba for tomorrow night's band concert, but you have a major test to study for. You cannot concentrate because of the noise.

8. Someone tells you that your friend was spreading rumors about you at the dance last night.

ANSWER KEYS TO REPRODUCIBLES

KINESICS (RC-37)

DIRECTIONS: Kinesics is the science of body language. It is a way of communicating mood, attitude, or information through body movements, posture, gestures, and facial expressions. Body language can send a message while a person is speaking, or it can send a silent message of its own. Read each example and write down what you think the body language is indicating.

Your sister, head lowered, shoulders slumped, drags herself off the basketball court after her team's last-second defeat in the playoffs. What does her body language indicate?

She is very disappointed over her team's loss.

Your teacher rolls his eyes, places his hand firmly on his hips, taps his foot, then fold his arms and waits because the class is disruptive. What does his body language say?

He is clearly annoyed at the class and wants their immediate attention.

Your mother quickly glares in your direction, wrinkles her forehead, and frowns when you tell an inappropriate joke at a family gathering. What does her body language indicate?

Your mother does not want you to tell the joke and is angry.

While talking to a friend, he looks around, shifts his position constantly, and taps his fingers. What does his body language tell you?

He is not paying attention and is anxious or nervous about something else.

While the teacher is talking, you slouch in your seat, yawn, and look at your watch. What does your body language indicate?

You are bored.

©1993 by The Center for Applied Research in Education

LISTEN TO ME! (RC-40)

DIRECTIONS: How much time do you spend listening during a typical school day? Look at the pie chart below and answer the questions.

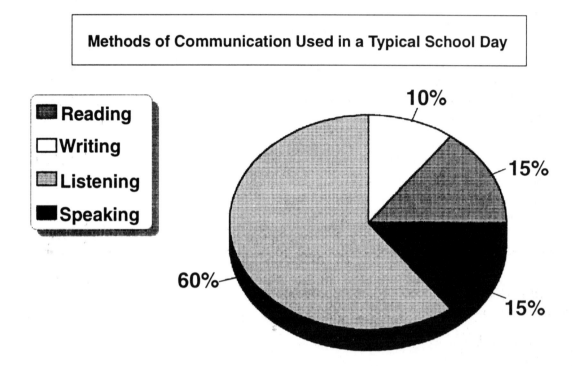

Methods of Communication Used in a Typical School Day

- Reading
- Writing
- Listening
- Speaking

10%
15%
60%
15%

©1993 by The Center for Applied Research in Education

1. According to the pie chart, approximately what percentage of the school day is spent listening?
   About 60% of the school day is spent listening.

2. Why do you think this is the case?
   Teachers will lecture, give directions, lead discussions; other students may respond to questions, or ask questions.

3. Based on this graph, why is it important to have good listening skills?
   Since more than half of the school day is spent listening, it is important to get accurate information and really hear what others are saying.

4. What types of problems can result from not listening well? Explain.
   You could miss important assignments or directions, misinterpret what others say, have inaccurate material from which to study, hurt your grade, interfere with class running smoothly, etc.

5. Give a specific example of a time you did not listen well in school.
   (Answers will vary.)

PASSIVE, AGGRESSIVE, OR ASSERTIVE? (RC-46)

©1993 by The Center for Applied Research in Education

DIRECTIONS: Write *aggressive, assertive,* or *passive* in the blank to the left to describe the response to each question.

<u>**aggressive**</u>   1. Can you help me with my book report? I won't get a chance to read the whole book.

      Why should I help you? You're too lazy! It's not my problem!

<u>**passive**</u>   2. Can I borrow your new outfit? I won't ruin it.

      Well...I didn't get a chance to wear it yet, but...well, okay.

<u>**assertive**</u>   3. I need to borrow $50 to pay a traffic ticket. How 'bout lending it to me?

      I'm really not able to lend you the money. I can't help you out.

<u>**assertive**</u>   4. Let's go to the mall and hang out tonight. There's nothing better to do.

      I don't want to go to the mall tonight. I'd prefer to go to the movies.

<u>**aggressive**</u>   5. Can I be on your team for basketball?

      No! You stink...besides, we have enough players already!

<u>**passive**</u>   6. Let's have a few beers—no one is home and they'll never find out.

      I'm not sure if that's such a good idea...but, okay, I guess it would be allright.

<u>**assertive**</u>   7. Let's skip school and go to the beach today.

      I'm not taking a chance like that. I'm going to school.

<u>**passive**</u>   8. Can I stay at your house for the weekend?

      Well...I was having a friend from my old neighborhood stay over, but okay...I guess so.

<u>**aggressive**</u>   9. Give me your homework to copy...I was on the phone all night.

      No, do your own work, you idiot!

<u>**assertive**</u>   10. Can you babysit for me this weekend?

      I made other plans with my friends. I won't be able to help you this particular weekend.

Call me Einstein but...
I'd say this is AGGRESSIVE!!

"I" STATEMENTS (RC-50)

DIRECTIONS: An "I" statement is a statement of your feelings that does not blame or judge the other person. The statement starts with "I feel…," "I want…," "I'm upset because…" Change the "You" statements below into "I" statements.

Suggested Answers:

"You" Statements	"I" Statements
You never call me when I ask you to!	*I wish we could talk on the phone more often.*
Will you turn down your stereo? I can't hear myself think!	*I have a difficult time concentrating when the stereo is so loud.*
Will you clean your room? I've asked you to do it five times!	*I get upset when I ask you to clean your room and it doesn't get done.*
You are so annoying when you tease me!	*I feel hurt when you make fun of me.*
Why don't you grow up and stop acting like a baby?!	*I wish we could have a more mature relationship.*
Will you stop interrupting me?	*I need to finish telling you about this without interruption.*
You're such a loud mouth!	*I feel uncomfortable when you yell at me.*
You can't play basketball, you stink! Go play on another team.	*I would rather we play on different teams today.*
It's your fault I got in trouble! Why did you have to tell on me?	*I'm angry that you didn't talk things out with me before going to Mom and Dad.*
You never listen when I give you directions!	*I need you to pay attention to the directions I give you.*
You always ignore me when your other friends are around!	*I feel left out when you exclude me from the conversation when others are around.*
You never let me do anything!	*I wish you trusted me to do more things.*
Why don't you do your own homework and stop copying mine?!	*I don't like it when you copy my homework.*
You are so moody sometimes!	*I feel uncomfortable when you react differently to me for no apparent reason.*
You never told us the assignment was due today! That's not fair!	*I don't remember being told about this assignment.*